Published in April 2024

Original Title: 80 Simple yet Powerful Lessons I've Learned in my 30s
Author and copyright: Bethany Platanella
Cover illustration: Francesca Cosanti
Graphic design: Francesca Cosanti
IBSN number: 979-8-9890068-2-3

First edition: April 2024

80 SIMPLE YET POWERFUL LESSONS I'VE LEARNED IN MY 30S

THAT HAVE MADE MY LIFE EASIER
(OR MAYBE I JUST CARE LESS)

BETHANY PLATANELLA

Life.

From the perspective of a single woman during the final year of her thrilling thirties.

One.

It's going to pass. Emotions are like everything in the universe, they expand and contract. They are not stationary nor are they solid.

Two.

Life is bigger than whatever you're going through at that moment.

Three.

Let him initiate.

Four.

Limit sun exposure.

Five.

Take Sundays to be slow.

Six.

Cats are the perfect companion for overly-independent, slightly-introverted and exploratory people.

Seven.

Asking the barista to mix salty and caramel popcorn at the movie theater will elevate your experience.

Eight.

Be open to pivots, professionally and personally.

Nine

Who you are will change a lot. Don't feel like you need to stay committed to the ways you've defined yourself. "I'm someone who needs to live by the ocean" might not be fundamentally who you are but rather *who you are at this period in your life.*

Ten.

Eat fruit
for breakfast.

Eleven.

Eat fruit for detox.

Twelve.

House plants and cut flowers will make you a happier person, which brings me to...

Thirteen.

The happier you are, the happier your plants.

Fourteen.

Flights on Friday the 13th and September 11 are usually cheaper.

Fifteen.

Invest in a cleaning person.

Sixteen.

Meditate. Even when you don't want to.

Seventeen.

Walk everywhere you can.

Eighteen.

Headphones
are
not
necessary
all the time.

Nineteen.

Be bored.
Sit with it.

Twenty.
Lift weights.

Twenty One.

Dijon mustard, with or without honey, makes an excellent salad dressing.

Twenty Two.

Take an edible once in a while.

Twenty Three.

Falling in love
is worth the
possible heartache.

Twenty Four.

If you live by the beach and you don't have a scooter, you're not getting the full experience.

Twenty Five.

Always carve out one day to ride a bike around a new place.

Twenty Six.

We are culturally conditioned to feel certain ways around certain people. Recognize it and refuse to succumb to it. No one outside of yourself has the right to dictate how you interpret life.

Twenty Seven.

You control
how you feel,
always.

Twenty Eight.

Quit smoking.
Now.

Twenty Nine.

Quit eating processed food. Now.

Thirty.

The body is a perfect mechanism that is built to heal itself. Trust it.

Thirty One.

You're not
"almost 40".
You're 38
until you're
39 until
you're 40.

Thirty Two.

Make game nights a thing.

Thirty Three.

Join a book club and read genres you wouldn't usually read.

Thirty Four

Listen to Crime & Punishment by Dostoyevsky on audio.

Thirty Five.

Read The Alchemist every few years.

Turn the phone off frequently and put it on Airplane Mode during the day when you travel.

Thirty Seven.
Move all electronics (phone, ipad, laptop) out of your room to sleep.

Thirty Eight.

Always bring wine, flowers or tea when visiting someone's house, especially for the first time.

Thirty Nine.

Speaking of, most people appreciate flowers for any occasion.

Morning silence is golden.

Forty One.

Get
massages.

Forty Two.

It's never too late to do it.

Forty Three.

Always carry lipstick.

Forty Four.

Invest in an elegant
pair of gold hoops.
If you're a man,
a fashionable watch.
It doesn't have to be
a Rolex, just
something cool and
classy.

Forty Five.

If there's a rooftop bar, have a drink at sunset.

Forty Six.

Wear more white.

Forty Seven

See your favorite piece of art, wherever it is in the world.

Forty Eight.

Hike as much as possible in as many places as possible.

Forty Nine.

Have a sweatshirt you love.

Fifty.

Buy a rug
you love.

Fifty One.

Sleep naked.

Fifty Two.

Have enough dishes to invite friends over for a meal. Otherwise you'll become a hermit.

Fifty Three

Introduce people you think might be a good fit, romantically, platonically or professionally.

Fifty Four.

You might start loving jazz. Embrace it.

Fifty Five.

Breathe and pay attention to the pattern.

Fifty Six.

Move in the direction of your interests. Even if it seems useless. Everything starts coming together.

Fifty Seven

When you're having a brain block, stop thinking and spend the afternoon in a museum.

Fifty Eight.

Choose to see the positive, even when it seems impossible.

Fifty Nine.

Support your friend's business in any way you can.

Sixty.

Wear cotton panties.

Sixty One.

Stretch
every day.

Sixty Two.

Check the bill before you pay it.

Sixty Three.

If he splits the check, write him off.

Sixty Four.

Wake up
before
the sun.

Sixty Five.

Book the aisle seat.

Sixty Six.

The quality of the hotel has the power to make all the difference.

Sixty Seven.

If no one can go with you, go on your own.

Sixty Eight.

Write in a gratitude journal until you no longer need to write in the gratitude journal.

Analyzing every single event to uncover the lesson will drive you crazy. It will soon become obvious, anyway.

A cashew
is actually a seed.

We all have the option to blame our parents. We all have the option not to.

Seventy Two.

Send postcards.

Seventy Three.

A face mask of honey and lemon juice will leave your skin bright and shiny.

Seventy Four.

Ingest raw, juiced turmeric each morning and you will be glowing within days.

Seventy Five.

Remove dairy. It will change your life.

Seventy Six

Most people have no idea how much better they could feel.

Seventy Seven.

Medjool dates are delicious when cold.

Feel your feelings and move the F on.

Seventy Nine.

Life is fast
and
beautiful.

Eighty.

When you trust, all goes well.

* 9 7 9 8 9 8 9 0 0 6 8 2 3 *